Spike's Crime Time

Clive Gifford

Illustrated by Mark Chambers

"This is Spike's Crime Time and I am Spike Nice." Spike loved to smile and show his white teeth on TV. But this time he looked grave as he held up a file.

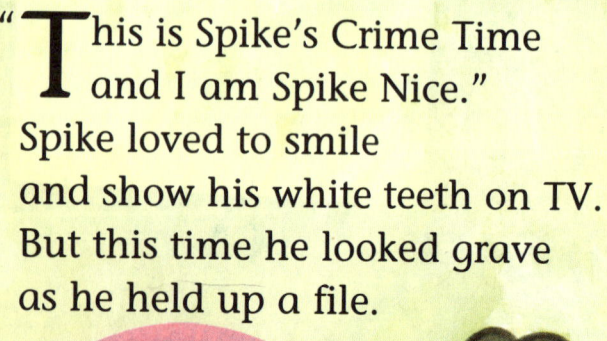

"There is a vile wave of crime on the rise, my friends. A criminal called The Viper is stealing bikes and kites. The theft of a blue and white striped kite was the last of his crimes.

These crimes rile me. Who could be such a *swine*? Here on Crime Time, we have an idea…"

Someone has stolen the letters o and e from each of these words from the story.

Can you put the letters back in their right places?

___ n ___

m ___ l ___

l ___ v ___ d

p h ___ n ___

p ___ l i c ___

s p ___ t t ___ d

3

"This film shows the prison escape of Mike Vine in County Pine. Vine is so agile, he can bend his bones and spine. He is a master of disguise and can become any shape or size. He slides through pipes, like a snake. That is why he is called The Viper!

He duped a dopey prison guard by becoming as thin as a pole. Then he vaulted over the prison wall and slipped into the night.

Vine escaped five days ago, the same time as the crimes began.

Our advice to you all is do not excite him, he might **bite**!"

What rhymes with these words? Look at these pictures for clues.

5

nice _____ _____ _____

alive _____ _____ _____

tone _____ _____ _____

pose _____ _____ _____

stole _____ _____ _____

"The Viper always wears lime green ties.
So if you spot him, phone **nine**, **nine**, **nine** – and win a prize. This has been Crime Time, with me, Spike Nice."

The Viper watched Crime Time from his hide-out.
He shared a wide pipe on a building site with a mole.

"The only crime of mine was to scare some horrible white mice. I never bite, or steal kites or bikes," he whined.

The mole smiled,
as he thought
The Viper was nice.

Can you put all these words from the story in alphabetical order?

rice

kite

_____

_____

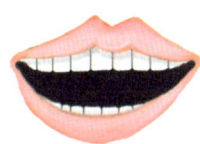

pipe

bite

_____

_____

file

time

_____

_____

nine

bikes

7

The Viper woke after a doze and spotted a note from the mole.

I know you did not steal all those kites and bikes. When digging holes in a garden last week, I spotted piles of kites hidden from sight. The garden belonged to the TV host, Spike Nice!

The Viper smiled. "I need gloves and my notebook. It is time to **STRIKE**! Spike Nice will pay for his crimes and give back the bikes and kites!"

He then slipped out of the pipe to look for the mole.

All these words are found in the story. Can you draw lines to link the pairs of words that rhyme?

hide   price

crime   hike

nice   nose

bike   prize

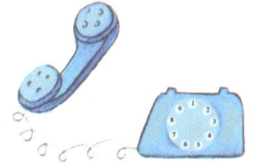

phone   time

rose   outside

size   alone

The Viper and mole dined on spiced chicken and rice.
Then they took a five-mile hike to the home of Spike Nice.

Twice, The Viper had to hide as people rode by.
And he froze when he saw a sign
"THE VIPER: WANTED ALIVE".

They reached the home of Spike Nice by five.
The Viper said,
"Mole, stay out here and hide."

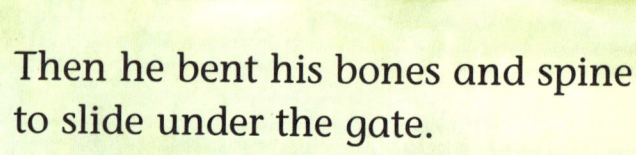

Then he bent his bones and spine to slide under the gate.

He posed as a garden hose to get past a gardener planting a rose.
Then he slid up a pipe and climbed into Spike's home.

Each group of letters below needs one more letter to form a word. Use one of the three letters The Viper is showing you to complete each word.

ite   ___ ___ ___ ___

prie ___ ___ ___ ___ ___

nte   ___ ___ ___ ___

nake ___ ___ ___ ___ ___

yu   ___ ___ ___

nie   ___ ___ ___ ___

The Viper was wide-eyed at what he saw inside. There were dozens of bikes of all sizes and types.

The Viper made notes for the police, as he spied all the bikes. Then he saw the pile of kites spotted by the mole from his hole.

The Viper saw one with blue and white stripes. "That was the kite they showed on Crime Time."

The Viper picked up the blue and white kite. "This will prove that Spike Nice **stole**. What a swine!"

bikes

 **Look at the kites and match each one with the word or phrase that describes it.**

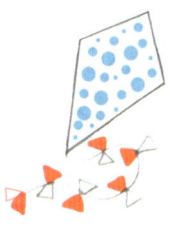

striped

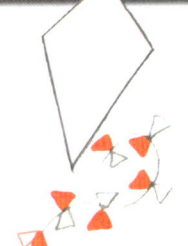

blue spots

lime green

white

biggest

smallest

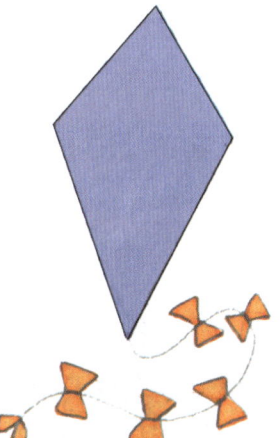

13

The Viper jumped when he turned to find Spike Nice at his side. The kite slipped from his hand as Spike GRABBED his lime tie. The Viper tried to slide free from Spike's vice-tight grip.

"Let me go, Spike, or you will pay the price!"

Spike showed him five white mice.

The Viper's spine turned to ice. He didn't like mice.

"If you don't whine, I'll hide my mice, along with your notes and gloves and the bikes and kites. Then I will take you to the police and get my prize."

Some of these words can have the letter i replaced by the letter o to make a new word. Colour in the kite if you can make a new word.

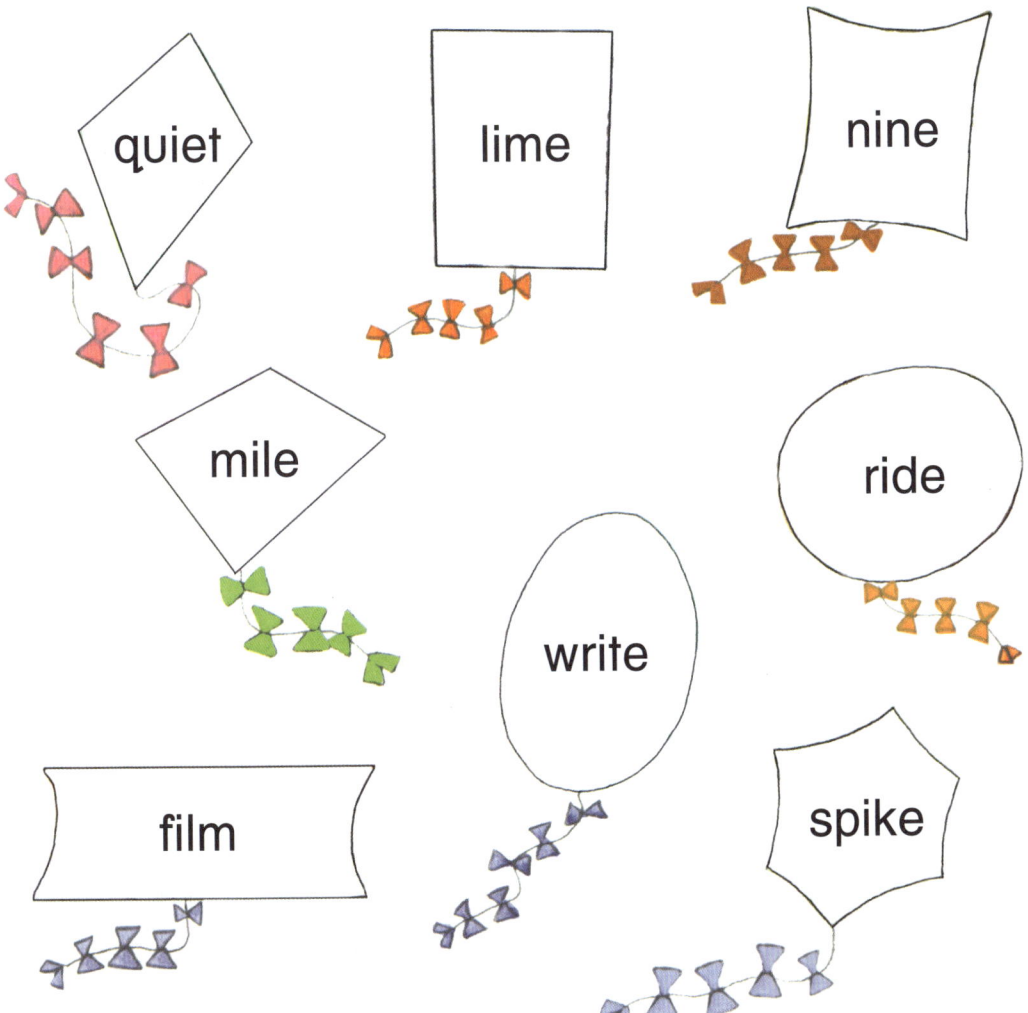

But PC Pope stood outside the home of Spike Nice. He spotted the loose kite now caught on a pipe. He called for back-up on his phone and then went in alone.

He hid and saw Spike frighten the Viper with his mice.

The Viper said, "I will tell the police about your lies and crimes."

"Ha, but who will the police think is telling lies?" replied Spike.

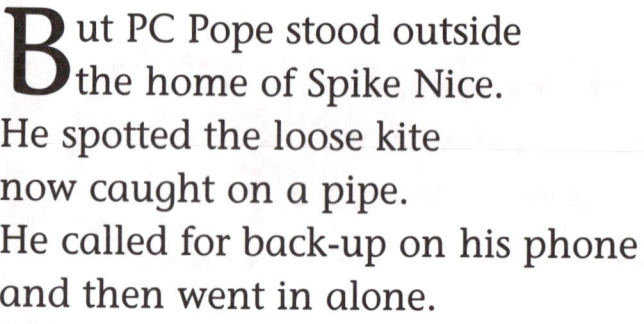

"Nice Spike from Crime Time or The Vile Viper? You are a **joke** and a **dope** and you have **no hope**."

You can make twelve words of more than two letters out of the word **police**. See how many of the others you can find. Two have been written out below.

PC Pope jumped out. "Aha, Mike Vine, also known as The Viper! You escaped from County Pine Prison, after scaring white mice."

"But mine was a tiny crime, not like Spike's, stealing all these kites and bikes."

PC Pope looked around and grabbed hold of the mice.

"I arrest you, Spike Nice, for stealing bikes and kites."

Spike tried to ride away on a stolen white bike.

But The Viper posed as a rope and wound round the spokes of Spike's bike.
"Now, *who* is the **dope** with **no hope**?" he smiled.

You are a reporter on the crime scene at the home of Spike Nice. Look at the picture opposite and add words to the sentences below to complete your report.

The Daily Chime

Crimes of Spike

By _____.

I am standing in the _ _ _ _ _ _ of Spike _ _ _ _.

The walls are painted _ _ _ _ _ _ and I can see _ _ _ _ kites.

The largest kite is bright _ _ _ _ _.

There are also _ _ _ _ _ _ bikes in the room.

The smallest is painted _ _ _ _.

What a bad man Spike is!

I am so pleased PC _ _ _ _ _ and The _ _ _ _ _ _ caught him.

19

"Stop whining, Nice.
Get used to County Pine prison life.
If you cannot do the time,
then do not do the crime.
Vile crimes against children – no one is
on your side," said a guard.

"Now be quiet, sit down
and eat your rice," said the cook.

After they dined, it was TV time
for the prisoners.

Spike liked watching TV, but soon he cried and wiped his eyes.

"Hi, this is The All-New Crime Time, with me, Mike 'Viper' Vine.
This is my wise friend, mole.
We are here to fight **crime!**"

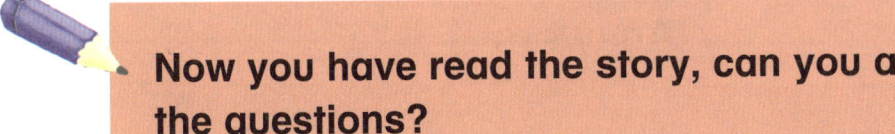

Now you have read the story, can you answer the questions?

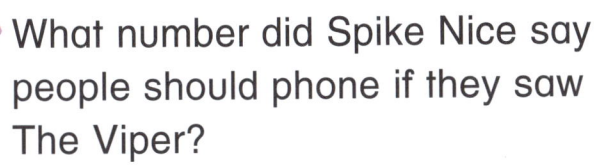

1. What number did Spike Nice say people should phone if they saw The Viper? _____

2. What was the real name of the man known as The Viper? _____

3. What was the name of the policeman who came to Spike Nice's house? _____

4. What colour was the tie worn by The Viper? _____

5. What did The Viper pose as to get past the gardener? _____

6. How many white mice did Spike have? _____

Answers

Page 3
one
mole
loved
phone
police
spotted

Page 5
dice, mice, rice
dive, five, hive
bone, cone, phone
hose, nose, rose
hole, mole, pole

Page 7
bikes
bite
file
kite
nine
pipe
rice
time

Page 9
hide → outside
crime → time
nice → price
bike → hike
phone → alone
rose → nose
size → prize

Page 11
site
price
note
snake
you
nice

22

Page 13

striped

blue spots

lime green

white

biggest

smallest

Page 15

spike ➜ spoke
nine ➜ none
mile ➜ mole
ride ➜ rode
write ➜ wrote

Page 17

pole, ice, lip, pile, cope, lie, oil, coil, pie, clip
(other possible words: epic, lop, lope as well as many others.)

Page 19

I am standing in the h o u s e of Spike N i c e.
The walls are painted w h i t e and I can see f i v e kites.
The largest kite is bright b l u e.
There are also t h r e e bikes in the room.
The smallest is painted r e d.
What a bad man Spike is!
I am so pleased PC P o p e and The V i p e r caught him.

Page 21

1. nine, nine, nine
2. Mike Vine
3. PC Pope
4. lime green
5. a garden hose
6. 5

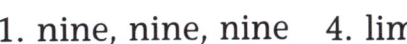

23

Published 2004
10 9 8 7 6 5 4 3 2

Letts Educational, The Chiswick Centre,
414 Chiswick High Road, London W4 5TF
Tel 020 8996 3333   Fax 020 8996 8390
Email mail@lettsed.co.uk
www.letts-education.com

Text, design and illustrations © Letts Educational Ltd 2004
Nelson handwriting font © Thomas Nelson

Book Concept, Development and Series Editor:
Helen Jacobs, Publishing Director
Author: Clive Gifford
Book Design: 2idesign Ltd, Cambridge
Illustrations: Mark Chambers, The Bright Agency

All rights reserved. No part of this publication may be reproduced, stored in a retrieval system, or transmitted, in any form or by any means, electronic, mechanical, photocopying, recording or otherwise, without the prior permission of Letts Educational.

British Library Cataloguing in Publication Data

A CIP record for this book is available from the British Library.

ISBN 978-1-84315-453-2

Printed in Italy

Colour reproduction by PDQ Digital Media Solutions Ltd, Bungay, Suffolk NR35 1BY